T0106206

MY CHILD IS
AUTISTIC

RENITHA TUTIN

authorHOUSE®

AuthorHouse™ UK Ltd.
500 Avebury Boulevard
Central Milton Keynes, MK9 2BE
www.authorhouse.co.uk
Phone: 08001974150

First published by AuthorHouse 12/28/2010

ISBN: 978-1-4567-7188-1 (sc)

For my beautiful boy.
Thank you for making me smile every day.

CONTENTS

CHAPTER ONE

HOPE

The purpose of this book is to give hope to parents of children on the autistic spectrum.

The first thing I remember after the horror and pain of being told that my son is autistic was the huge sense of responsibility I felt to somehow reach this child. I remember the million questions going through my mind. How would I get help for him? Who would teach him? (I certainly wasn't equipped to do so.) Would he ever know me and love me? Would I ever know him? How was I going to tell others that he is autistic? And how was I going to watch their faces as they struggled to find something appropriate to say to me in response? How was I going to give up all the dreams that I had for this little person who had come into my life? How was I going to be the amazing parent that I had hoped and dreamed I would be?

The various specialists I met after the initial diagnosis were all very sympathetic, but they were all grim – as if this were the worst news you could possibly give a parent. At the time it did seem as though it was. At the time there seemed to be nothing positive about my son getting this diagnosis. Yes, the specialists were all kind and supportive, but there was no doubt in my mind that they felt sorry for us, that they believed that there was nothing but years of struggle and hardship ahead for us. They were very clear that life would be difficult. I think they felt they needed to put this across. They needed to make sure that we would not be in denial and have any false illusions that life would be rosy or happy.

We were told that there was a course we could go on. It lasted a few weeks for a couple of hours each week. They were kind, the people who ran the course. They tried to provide as much information as they could about autism – the difficulties and problems we would face. Every meeting was depressing and spelled out a life of hardship with examples of scenarios we would encounter. It seemed important to them that we accept what was inevitable, for ourselves as well as our child. That seemed to be the best way forward.

I am not an expert but simply a parent who feels, dreams, hopes and fears. Now my son is eight. We are still only at the beginning of our remarkable journey, but I want to tell you that it does not have to be doom and gloom if you get the diagnosis that your child is autistic. I want to tell you that yes, there will be difficult times, but there will be very happy and exciting ones too. I want to tell you that your child is not less of a person just because he is autistic. I want to tell you to keep hoping. I want to tell you to keep dreaming. I want to tell you to listen to the 'experts', take it all in, follow the instructions that work for you, but above all, keep the hope and go for all the dreams you planned for your child before you found out that he was autistic.

I am aware, as with 'normal' children, that every child is different. This account does not mean that I think that every child diagnosed on the autistic spectrum could achieve what my little boy has achieved. I have met, have read about, and have seen children on the spectrum who are locked away in their minds. I know there are thousands of parents out there doing anything and everything to set them free. This book is simply about how we came from a diagnosis of doom and gloom to one where we now see endless possibilities for our son.

I had no intention of writing a book on autism, as I am just a parent of an autistic child, and perhaps I have been lucky in how my son has developed. But then again, perhaps it was the combination of things that we have done that has made life happy again. Something happened a couple of days ago that motivated me to start this book. We were at the zoo entrance queuing to go in, my husband, my son and myself, and there was a mum with her son looking very distressed. She was upset that the queue was so long, and she asked us if she could cut in as her son was upset. Not a very 'English' thing to do, but one look at her face and I saw all the emotions, the pain, the anxiety that once were a permanent feature on my own face. Her son looked a couple of years younger than ours. He was agitated, unable to stand still, and she was constantly trying to hold on to him and calm him. It took me back a few years, and I just wanted to reach out to her and say something reassuring.

I couldn't find the words. I could only tell her that she could jump the queue. It was so obvious to me that her son was on the autistic spectrum. It was so obvious that she was upset and embarrassed about the situation. It was so obvious she was grateful that somebody was kind to her.

At that moment it dawned on me how difficult it is to help anyone in that position. How difficult it must have been for anyone to help me when I was struggling, upset, and angry with the world for not helping. What could I say to her? I could tell her that I understood – that I had been through it all. But could I really do that? What if she was not at the point yet where she had got a diagnosis and accepted that he was on the spectrum?

If she did already have a diagnosis, maybe I could reassure her by pointing to my son and telling her it would get better, but how could I, when I did not know that for sure? I did what everyone did to me when they were the observers. I just watched the child, recognised his mum was struggling, and did nothing.

That was the day I decided that maybe I could write this book and maybe it could help others who needed hope. Maybe things that had worked for us could work for other parents of children with autism, so they could try them out rather than feeling they must merely accept that nothing can be done.

I shall spend the next couple of chapters explaining a little about our son and what we went through at the start of this journey. I expect many of you will be able to relate to some of the things we experienced and felt. Some of you will say that there are no similarities between our son and your child, but I am guessing the emotions you feel will be similar to ours. The later chapters will be about how we decided to proceed with the advice and the information we had. I hope that, even for those of you with different experiences and hurdles to face with your children, this book helps you deal with some of the questions and choices you are faced with. I believe that every child is different and there are no right or wrong choices, just a whole lot of decisions to be made and very little information for guidance. So here's my effort to try to fill in that information gap a little.

CHAPTER TWO

ACCEPTANCE

Those who have had a child diagnosed for anything know about the pit-in-the-stomach fear when it first occurs to them that their child is different – that sick feeling in your stomach that tells you that no matter how many ways you try to find excuses to deny the fact that your child is different, you will eventually have to face it.

People ask me when I knew that my son was autistic. I knew within the first few weeks of his birth. I remember thinking, 'It really shouldn't be this hard.' But of course, any doctor or midwife or parent would tell you that you are just tired or overwhelmed if you express this concern after just having a baby. They will suggest that you are suffering from post-natal depression. Some will look at you with mild annoyance, because they are thinking that you are just complaining and not taking it in your stride. I had a really easy pregnancy. I had read tons of books on babies and what to expect. Nothing prepared me for the nightmare of parenthood of an autistic child.

Now, of course not all autistic children react the same way when they are babies. Some are quite placid and even easy babies. There are no clues until they are a little bit older, when they start showing signs with their lack of communication, eye contact, social skills. Then it becomes apparent. We were not so lucky. My child screamed, and screamed, and screamed. He screamed when he was not carried. He screamed the second he realised he was hungry. There was never a build-up of grumbling, because when he was hungry, it was sudden and then continuous until a bottle was put in his mouth. Oh yes, he had to be bottle-fed as he couldn't breastfeed, but I will come to that later.

He would scream four or five times in the night, sometimes for milk, sometimes, I think, because he had nightmares. I believed he had nightmares, because sometimes nothing could calm him down when he woke up screaming, and he could scream for as long as an hour. His eyes would look around wildly, terrified, unable to focus on me, and he would fling himself around the room hysterically. I tried leaving the room, staying in the room, speaking soothingly, holding him. Nothing worked. The only thing I was ever able to do was to watch him and prevent him from hurting himself when he hurled himself around. When he calmed down, probably out of sheer exhaustion, he would cling on to me until he fell asleep again. Somehow, no matter how deep in sleep he was, he would know when I put him down in his cot. He slept on me for the first two years of his life. It had to be this way, as it was the only way for him to get a decent amount of sleep before the next feed or the next nightmare. It was the only way I could stop him from crying hysterically all night and prevent him from hurting himself.

I think it all started to go wrong from the day he was born. I had a Caesarean, as the doctors lost his heartbeat trace when I was almost fully dilated. He came out screaming, seemingly a fine and healthy child. The three nights I stayed in the hospital were anything but fine. He seemed unable to breastfeed. I remember many nurses trying to help me. Some seemed kind, feeling sorry for the first-time mother who had no idea what to do. Some were kind, but a little aggressive, telling me not to give up, as mother's milk was clearly the best thing for my son. The pressure not to fail at the starting line of my son's life was huge. But I did fail. He simply was not able to suck. Later I remember reading somewhere that the absence of breastfeeding increases the risk of autism. There are theories that suggest that autism could be caused by the lack of breastfeeding, but I wonder if the reverse is more likely. Perhaps babies are already autistic and cannot breastfeed. Breastfeeding, I have read, is a more complex kind of sucking than drinking from a bottle. They need to use their jaws with skill to get the milk out. My son always struggled with coordination, and I am sure it was beyond him to breastfeed.

Nobody even considered autism at the time. Why would they? I don't think it is even something that nurses and midwives are trained to consider. It must have been my fault for not trying hard enough. He screamed through the night. I would be sent to the 'quiet room' in the hospital to express milk so as not to wake up any other parents. He had a shrill scream. My husband and I still shudder when we hear a baby cry. Our son didn't do anything quietly. Everything was louder, shriller, more hysterical than other babies.

There was one kind midwife who did not just stick to her training of using guilt to persuade new mothers to breastfeed. She simply said to me that perhaps my child could not breastfeed for some reason and I should give myself a break and bottle-feed him and not feel guilty. So, for any of you out there who have been beating yourself up and blaming yourselves for 'failing' your child at the beginning, get rid of that guilt. It is not your fault. Nobody is to blame.

There were other signs. Some people noticed how our son screamed so much when he was a baby. Some made nasty comments. Some just laughed and tried to make jokes to ease the situation, although it used to amaze me how they thought a joke could drown out our child's high-pitched screams and help us. I remember being in a post-natal group and being the only mother there who had to get up and walk around rocking her baby the whole time. All the other babies just slept in their pushchairs, gurgled in their mothers' arms, or lay around awake taking in everything. I remember looking in amazement at those babies. I remember those other mothers looking at me with pity. But of course, no one was able to say anything or try to give any reason as to why my son was so difficult. If they had done so, I would have been horrified that the torture my son was putting me through was because of a disability. But the thing is, it would have been easier to realise that and deal with it rather than struggle as I did – not knowing why, feeling alone, feeling fear, and wasting precious time not doing everything I could to help my son.

As I mentioned earlier, my husband and I got very little sleep when my little boy was a baby, and we were permanently exhausted. I am sure we came across to many people as parents who just could not adjust to a different lifestyle. The 'helpful' comments we got from older people were based on a sample of one or two babies they had experienced in their lives. Everyone had something to say about the 'difficult times' they had when they had babies. No one really listened to how difficult a time we were having. Everybody wanted to believe that everything was all right. The alternative was too difficult for them to admit or suggest to us. All of this is because autism is seen as the end of a happy future. So who in their right mind would want to suggest it to new parents?

The most difficult part may be to diagnose and accept autism. I believe the sooner this is done, the sooner you can start to try to find solutions for your child. (Of course, you may need to argue and fight with various people to get this diagnosis.) For a normal child, it appears that the first six years are incredibly important for their development. Why should it be any different for an autistic child? I believe it is vital to get an early diagnosis, and anyone in a position to help a parent receive this diagnosis should do everything they can. Unfortunately, there seems to be a common view that children should not be labelled, based on the theory that it is counter-productive. Some experts appear reluctant to give parents the information that they believe, or at least suspect, to be true.

As my son got older, it started to become obvious to us that he was somewhere on the autistic spectrum, even though others still insisted he was developing fine. He was saying a few words. He was making some eye contact. When he was happy, he had the most disarming smile and infectious laugh. To many people, seeing those things was enough for them to confidently dismiss our fears about the possibility that our child was on the spectrum. What they did not see was that the words he used were random. He was not really attempting to communicate as other toddlers were trying to do. His eye contact was mainly with me, and only when he felt like doing it. He rarely even looked up when anybody else spoke, and often it was very difficult to get his attention.

He never played with toys as they should be played with. He would fiddle with them, or hide them, or simply ignore them. He would scream if the laws of physics defied him. For example, if a pencil would not stand on its tip when he tried to make it do so, he would be furious and would scream inconsolably for a full five minutes. Even after he accepted this, after watching it happen a hundred times, he could not use this new-found information to work out that another object, such as a pen, would suffer the same fate if he tried to stand it up.

He would not play with other children or seek them out. He did not even seem to notice them. When we went to parties, he would be the child in the corner, looking at a blade of grass, oblivious to all the fun and games and laughter going on around him.

He was finally diagnosed as severely autistic after turning three; I think this was because he chose not to respond to anything or show interest in anything during the various tests. We were told that he should go to a special school. He received a Statement of Special Educational Needs (SEN), and we were advised again at that point that mainstream school would not be good for him. I was against this idea, as I truly believed that he behaved differently with me. I believed that all the hours I spent carrying him when he screamed, letting him fall asleep on me because he could never be put down, talking to him all the time, that all of this made me special to him and would give me a connection to him that I could use to help him. I also believed that putting him in a special school, although in a way easier (since the pressure to fit in would be removed), would hold him back and not push him to be 'normal.'

So I started reading about everything I could do. The first thing, of course, would be to find a mainstream school that would take him.

CHAPTER THREE

SCHOOL

Finding a school that we liked was challenging. We visited a few, and it was obvious that a small, friendly school was the key. At every school, I would ask the person taking us around about special needs, and they all answered positively about how they had a SENCo (Special Educational Needs Coordinator) and all children were welcomed. When pushed a little further about what they knew about autism or how many autistic children they had, most of the time we got a vague response that showed very little experience or understanding of autistic children. Also, in some of the schools, I got the impression that SAT results were the thing they were most proud of, and often that made me feel that they would not be too pleased for my child to bring the scores down. The general impression of our visits led me to believe that there is very little knowledge, training, or experience regarding dealing with autistic children in these schools.

My husband and I were very wary about this. While my son was being diagnosed, he was going to a nursery and a preschool. The nursery had no idea that he was on the autistic spectrum. We even approached them a few times to tell them we thought he was autistic, and each time they dismissed it.

The preschool was worse in the sense that they recognised that there was something different about him. However, rather than helping him in any way, they referred to him as the 'naughty boy'. I know this because in the summer before he was to start school, I was in a play area with my son. I saw a couple of boys from his preschool, and they pointed at my son and said, 'Look, that is the naughty boy.' I told them that it was an unkind thing to say and asked them why they said it. They told me that was how the preschool teachers referred to him.

I had helped out a couple of times at preschool, and, yes, he was a handful. He would deliberately drop the beads, paper, or glitter they were using for artwork all over the floor. He would ignore them when they spoke to him. He would not sit still when the kids had their snack break. He would often wet himself. The preschool teachers would just shout or sigh at him, but they had absolutely no idea how to deal with him. I think they just put it down to bad parenting and to him being a spoilt child.

So, these experiences made us second guess whether we should go against the specialists' advice at the time. The lack of knowledge of autism and how to deal with it in schools made us wonder if he would be worse off if we pushed the issue.

We were very lucky though. We found this wonderful little school where the SENCo and the Reception teacher were happy to meet with us to discuss taking our son. The Reception teacher herself was actually interested in autism, and she came across as bright and cheery and full of hope and optimism. She did not even think it would be an issue to take him, as by then we had a Statement that provided for twenty-five hours one-to-one time with a teaching assistant. I think this meeting was the first time I had actually felt hopeful since the diagnosis. Her classroom assistant was equally enthusiastic. It was not because they did not understand how difficult it would be. They knew, because we gave them the lengthy diagnosis and Statement report, which detailed all his problems very clearly. I had been depressed reading this report, and yet these two women were happy to take him on. The SENCo and the head teacher had no issues either as long as the teachers were happy.

The school was in charge of recruiting the one-to-one assistant provided by the Statement who would aid them with my son for twenty-five hours a week. They chose perfectly. This woman had never taught an autistic child before. She had no training and was not an expert. She was young, had some experience with children, but not with special needs children. It worried me at the beginning. Every day in the first few weeks when I went to pick him up, I dreaded what they would say to me. Every day I expected them to tell me that they had tried their best, but it was not working, and I should put him in a special school.

But they never did. There were issues and problems, but they let me know about them and we dealt with them. In a way, I think it was the best thing possible that his one-to-one teacher was not an expert. She was surprised at how excited the teacher and I were one day when my son held a pencil and drew a letter (badly) on the page. I remember her looking bewildered and saying, 'You are happy with this?' She felt that he could do better. She pushed him to do better. She made me believe he could do better. The class teachers were the same. They corrected the bad behaviour without judgement. They were aware that many things were difficult for him. They never let him just take himself off into a corner to do nothing (something he often did in preschool and nursery). They did things like inviting me into the classroom every day in that first week to take him to the toilet because he was afraid of the hand-dryer. I had by then found a way to talk to him that he would listen to (see chapter 7), and they let me be a part of their 'team' to help him to fit into school. It was as if there was a conspiracy to prove that he could stay in mainstream school.

That Reception year set the bar for the rest of the years that have followed to date. His wonderful one-to-one teacher had to leave for personal reasons, but she still comes around to visit us, and I can see how proud she is of him for what he is achieving. She was a huge part of his adapting to and fitting into mainstream school.

The Reception class teacher decided to explain to all his classmates how he was different. She did this well. It made me think that the best way forward was for everyone to know that he is on the spectrum. So much better for them to understand why he was the way he was, rather than just to think he was a 'naughty boy.'

The next one-to-one teacher he had – and still has to this day – is also fabulous. She is playing a huge role in his life now, and I hope he has her for a long time to come.

The school made a huge difference to the level of our expectations. Every year they would push him to achieve what the other kids in the class did. Of course, there were and still are things that he struggles with. In later chapters I will discuss what they were and how we dealt with them. My point here is that getting the right school for your child is important (whether it be a special school or mainstream school). Getting people who really care and want to see him succeed is crucial. But most of all, having people who are positive, who do not see autism as the end of the line, is vital.

Of course, none of this would have been possible without a Statement. There is no way any teacher, however much she wanted to help him, could have the patience, the time, and the energy to deal with my son's very special demands, as well as a whole classroom of other kids. This is yet another reason why it is so important to get that diagnosis early.

A year after he was in school, it became very clear to me that we made the right decision when we put him in mainstream school. It was a risk to go against the experts and to follow our instincts at the time, but I now know we made the right decision.

One summer holiday after his first year at school, I enrolled him in a day club with other kids who had special needs. I was desperate for a break. The people running the centre were lovely and knowledgeable. The place was nice and safe, and they had a one-to-one adult-to-child ratio for my son. I could not have faulted the staff and the way it was run for anything. I had explained to my son that he would be dropped off and that he should do what they asked him to do just as he did in school. (We explain everything in detail, as you will read in a later chapter.) He was not anxious when I left him because there were so many things of interest there to stimulate him.

I came back to a very happy child, but after that day I will never put him in a place like that again. He was happy, and the staff was happy. However, when I picked him up, he was sitting in a chair, fiddling with some toy, with food stains down his clothes and wearing huge ear muffs. Apparently, he had complained about the noise, had put the ear muffs on, and would not take them off the whole time. He had refused to do anything and just spent his time wandering around and fiddling with everything. He had wet himself and had food all down his front after eating the packed lunch I left for him.

Oddly enough, the staff was actually quite pleased with him. They said he was a lovely boy and they enjoyed having him. However, to me he seemed to have regressed in that short time (not permanently of course). His whole attitude was one of being unable to do anything. At school he would have had no choice. He would have got his hands dirty and helped with the dough that made cookies in the centre that day. At school he would have been reminded to go to the toilet many times. For a long time, he didn't seem to know when he needed to go to the toilet, but he stayed dry most days in school simply because he was periodically told to go. At school there are no ear muffs. At school he would have had to sit down, and his attention would have been called back over and over again to the subject being discussed at the time.

He asked for ear muffs when we got home, and there was a lot of screaming and tears before he realised that there was no point in asking for them again. (Chapter 9 discusses how we later were able to desensitise him.)

I know that it was difficult for the staff in the day club to connect with my son in just one day, and of course in a special school, the staff would have a bond with the child they see every day. However, I believe that my son would do as little as possible if he could get away with it, and he has always needed to be pushed to do or learn anything. I also believe that watching other kids interact has helped him to copy 'acceptable behaviour'. So for him, mainstream school, where all the kids are expected to conform and get on with things, was exactly what he needed. This of course would not necessarily be the case for all children on the spectrum as some, depending on their personalities and individual needs, would possibly thrive with more specialist care.

Another reason we were keen on him going to mainstream school was the hope that he would eventually be able to cope and mix in society and maybe even one day hold down a job and be independent. To put him in special school at the start, in a way would possibly make it harder for him to integrate into society when he became older. We were also hoping that if he was surrounded by kids who are 'normal', he might eventually notice them and might even learn to fit in. I hoped against hope at the time that he would make some friends too. For a long time, he just tolerated the other children. The teachers put down 'playing with a friend' as one of his targets and often would encourage him to play. Eventually he would play games like tag, and if pushed by teachers, he would take part in more structured games.

There were, of course, the kids who knew instinctively that he was different and that he struggled with certain things. I would notice in the playground after school that they would taunt him sometimes about subjects he was sensitive about, just to get a reaction. More on this later.

There have been disagreements between my son and a few kids in his class. Sometimes it was because he decided for some reason that they were not a 'good' child. Sometimes it was because he enjoyed winding them up and watching them react. Sometimes it was the other child winding him up. He has never been allowed to get away with anything, but there is always more time and effort allocated to explaining things to him because of his Statement. There is always the option to take him out of the class when it becomes necessary to calm him down or to speak to him in a peaceful setting.

To date he is managing to keep up with the kids in his class thanks to the one-to-one help he has received. We never dared hope he would even learn to write when he went to school. We worked hard with the teachers, but we did not know if it would work. At the last Statement review, his teachers were saying that they thought he might even cope fine in secondary school, something that until last year we never thought possible. It is wonderful to be surrounded by hope.

Of course, secondary school and puberty will bring a whole host of problems, and children on the spectrum are said to struggle most at this age. But we will deal with it (and perhaps write another book) when the time comes.

CHAPTER FOUR

MUSIC

As soon as my son was diagnosed, I went out and read every single book I could find on autism. There are so many suggestions in the material out there, from the right foods, methods of teaching children using pictures, removing electronic stimulation, drugs, music therapy, to art; the list goes on. There are also scientific discussions, studies, and research about the brains of autistic people. What I understood from everything I had read (rightly or wrongly) was that it all boiled down to the way my son's brain was wired. I decided to ignore the impact of foods, as my son eats healthily (discussed in a later chapter), and I saw no reason to change something that was actually working by removing certain food groups. I rejected the idea of drugs (despite his violent temper tantrums), as we understand so little about autism, and the idea of pumping his system with drugs without knowing their full impact seemed a little scary to me.

Our brains are continuously changing and developing; I could see no reason why my son's brain (albeit an autistic one) shouldn't be able to do the same. The information I looked at described the relationship between the left and right hemispheres of the brain and how they are connected by white matter called the *corpus callosum.*

In this chapter I will set out my understanding of the two hemispheres and how I believe that their working together has a huge impact on the ability to perceive and react to the world.

The left and right hemispheres of the brain have different functions, and their only connection is a thick white band called the *corpus callosum.* The left brain is understood to deal with logic, analysis, and rationality, while the right brain is the intuitive, imaginative, 'arty' side of the brain.

Two questions arose in my mind when I was doing all this reading. Was the problem of autism caused by one hemisphere being weaker than another? Or was it caused by the connection between the brain hemispheres being weak? Which would be the weaker hemisphere for an autistic child?

Symptoms of autism are supposed to include impairments in language and communication, difficulty in reading facial expressions, the inability to show empathy, and narrow and repetitive communication and behaviour. This to me seemed to relate to both hemispheres. The left hemisphere is needed to understand complex sentences and verbal communication. It is rule orientated, dealing with problem solving and logic, whereas the right side characteristics include understanding emotions, having the ability to arrange pictures in a specific pattern, seeing the whole and then details, and enjoying touching and feeling objects to learn.

My son seemed to have strong and weak characteristics for both sides of the brain, so I concluded that it was more likely that autism – his variety at least – was largely down to the link (the *corpus callosum*) being weak, rather than a problem with the development of one of the hemispheres.

It seemed to me that any task that we perform can be broken down into right and left brain components. For example, with everyday conversation, the right hemisphere would visualize the message being conveyed. It may move quite quickly from one picture to another, sometimes randomly, and lose the thread of the conversation. Feelings are attached to these pictures but may not be easy to decipher and convey. The left hemisphere's function here would be to process the words heard using logic and objectivity, and there would be a methodical process to respond verbally or with symbols or numbers.

There were also various books and articles I read that suggested that in people with autism, the parts of the brain that perform complex analysis appear less likely to work together than in people who are not on the spectrum. So getting around the failure of the two parts of the brain to 'talk' to each other effectively could be the key to helping my son.

The obvious question was what could be done to strengthen the link between the two hemispheres. I remembered hearing somewhere (probably a medical drama on TV!) that playing a musical instrument was the only thing that caused significant activity in both the left and right hemispheres at the same time. I read several articles about this, and they seemed to suggest that playing a musical instrument starts with the eyes passing on the information it sees to the brain and stimulating both the logical and creative areas of the brain. It stands to reason that if an autistic child could learn to play an instrument, it might strengthen the *corpus callosum*, enhancing communication between the two sides of the brain. Indeed, some articles suggested that children who started practising an instrument before the age of seven had a thicker *corpus callosum*.

All this was very exciting and hopeful, so when at four years old my son still had no meaningful communication and still had tantrums, I decided to try to teach him to play the piano. Fortunately, I play the piano myself and did not have to inflict this task on a qualified piano teacher.

It was a very difficult task to begin with. Just to get him to sit on the piano stool took some effort. He would fidget, bang his fingers randomly on notes, kick the piano, pull the book off and fling it across the room, try to shut the lid of the piano (often on my hands!), and most days he had the concentration span of a goldfish. I started by trying to get him to sit at the piano for a minute. I got a book for very young children with pictures, and I made up stories about how we needed to find and play the note middle C with his right and left hands. I would have to physically move his right and left hands over the note and point to the note drawn in the book (and sometimes grab him as he tried to escape from the stool).

He would often have a tantrum and resist at the beginning, but then for some inexplicable reason he started to look at the notes in the book and try to play them. Thinking about it now, it probably just became routine in his mind – something he was forced to do – so he would do it as quickly as possible just to get it over and done with. At the age of four and five, we never sat at the piano for more than ten minutes (including time for tantrums). I was not always patient, and this was a mistake. I would shout at him sometimes, and this would set him back. Then I would have to cajole him and start the whole process again the next time.

If it seems too daunting to teach an autistic child to learn an instrument, a point to note is that it does not have to be taught in the conventional way. What I mean is that if it seems that there is too much to take in at once at the start, then do not do it all at once. For example, if I were teaching a 'normal' child, I would teach him or her, the theory of music at the same time. I would teach the child about rhythm (the number of beats in each note, in each bar, etc.). I would explain and help the child say the words 'treble clef' and 'bass clef' and perhaps teach the child to draw the notes he or she was learning on the music stave. When the child played, I would make him or her use the correct fingering. I would make him or her observe rests and hold notes for the correct length of time.

With my son, I just went straight to the beginner's piano book and taught him to play the notes straightaway on the piano. He would not have listened to any of the theory or taken it in. He would not have been able to draw a single note. I did not even try to teach him about rhythm, or expression, or the Italian terms. With him, part of the teaching was about keeping him interested and focussed. I waited two years before I even thought about making him play anything to time. It did not seem to make a difference when he did learn it, as he has no problem counting to time now as well as playing the notes. So keeping it simple to start with was the key (pardon the pun), but then once he got it, there was no reason to avoid adding other complications. As in everything else, autistic children need things broken down into manageable parts. They need not to be overwhelmed with the whole. I think that if there seems to be too much to do at once, their brains just shut down and they do not even try.

I look back now, and I cannot believe that the child I knew at four can today sit and play pieces on the piano. He can even play pieces from memory. He can play Grade 3 pieces now at the age of eight. Practising is something we do nearly every day, but not for very long, as he sees it as hard work. He has recently shown pleasure about 'performing' in front of other people, as he is beginning to appreciate praise and applause. I firmly believe that one of the main reasons he has come along in leaps and bounds in understanding and interpreting the world since the age of four is because of playing the piano.

CHAPTER FIVE

GROSS MOTOR SKILLS

We noticed that our son's coordination was never really good from the time he was a toddler. He never crawled and went straight to walking. Some experts see this as missing a developmental milestone, missing an important sequence in his growth. He used to be very clumsy until the age of four. He would fall from a standing-still position. He could not hop or skip or jump. It was impossible for him to sit on a bicycle, let alone ride one.

The only solution we could think of was to take him to different soft-play areas. At the age of two we started with the smaller ones, like the ones full of colourful balls with padded floors and steps. He would not move from one spot the first time we took him there, and he seemed very disturbed by the colours and textures around him. He needed to be guided through every tunnel, space, and step.

These places are usually very colourful and noisy, and I think this was an issue for him too. So we did it for a few minutes at a time to begin with. It was here that I realised that it was possible to get him slowly used to things he initially found overwhelming. As long as we did not leave it too long between visits (sometimes we would go three or four times a week), he seemed to be able to stay longer and longer. Once he got over whatever it was that frightened him to begin with, he would just run wildly and very quickly through the whole soft-play area. He would fall and crash into things, and as long as he didn't feel pain, he would get up and carry on. If he did get hurt, there would be an almighty tantrum that could easily last for half an hour, and we would have to hurriedly take him home. This obviously was an expensive 'therapy,' as often we would pay for an hour and only be 'allowed' to stay for five minutes.

But it was worth it as his coordination definitely improved. I would have to chase him around and play with him, as he couldn't make friends or play with other kids. So we would play on his terms, and I was happy to do that as long as he got better with his movements, and he did.

In my son's school they offer a half-an-hour club twice a week where they work on developing gross motor skills. They work very hard through a list of things like balance (walking on lines, low beams), skipping, catching and throwing balls, and so on. I have seen him improve at all these things over the years from practising, but it has to be practising without long breaks in between to be effective.

The biggest change in his movements and coordination I have to say came from doing taekwondo. I had read Luke

Jackson's book *Freaks, Geeks and Asperger's Syndrome*, and he talked about doing taekwondo. I remember thinking that maybe when my son was older we might attempt it. When my son was four and in school, I was worried about the possibility of him being bullied for being different as he got older. Learning a martial art seemed like a good solution to that. I also wondered whether, besides helping him with his coordination (if he could do it), it would help strengthen the right brain-left brain link. After all, it is a sequence of movements that needs to be memorised, visualised, and replayed in a certain order.

Looking and finding a suitable instructor was not easy. I had been to two martial arts instructors and asked them if they would take my son. The reaction from the first one was confusion, as he did not understand what it meant to be autistic. The reaction from the second one was not encouraging; he seemed not to want to say no, but he made it clear that it would be very difficult in a large class for someone like my son to cope and keep up.

The third instructor I met was like a dream come true. She did not even blink when I asked her if she would take on a child on the autistic spectrum. At the time I wondered if she understood how hard he would be. She suggested he take the two free classes they offer to beginners to see how he got on. I asked her if we could just come to sit and watch for as long as it took for him to feel comfortable enough to join in. She did not have a problem with this. She made everything so easy and so hopeful from the start.

Amazingly, he did join in after sitting and watching just two classes. He used to struggle to stand still when it was required. He would hide behind the curtains in the class before it started, while all the other children ran around playing. His instructor would have to coax him out. He often struggled to listen and be quiet, and she would patiently remind him each time to listen when he babbled on about something while she was speaking. He definitely struggled with the simple movements that the other children picked up so easily. He was comical to watch. The reason he stayed on despite all this was that his instructor seemed almost oblivious to all that he could not do. 'Seemed' is the key word here. She was very aware what he could not do, but she treated him just like everyone else. There was no laughing at him, and this was sometimes incredibly hard not to do! There was no obvious attention paid to him, but she did help him by taking the time to explain very clearly and slowly everything he needed to do. She would move his arms, hands, and legs to help him if he just did not understand her instruction like the other kids did.

She told him off in the same way she would the other kids, but, equally, she encouraged and praised him when he worked hard and managed to do the simplest things. When he was seven, he started to really enjoy it. He adores his instructor and never wants to let her down. I think she has been a huge inspiration to him, and because of her I think he believes that with hard work anything is possible. He talks now about how difficult he found taekwondo in the beginning. He still struggles with any new movement he learns and is certainly not a 'natural.' Some moves seem particularly difficult for him – anything that involves a turn or an angle, for example. He probably has to practise harder than the average child to learn something new, but once he has got it and it becomes routine (and this may come after quite a few attempts and tears of frustration), he seems to remember it forever. He talks about how he will work very hard to get his black belt one day. It may take a long time for him, but he is determined.

He even does gradings (tests) now, where he is assessed to see if he can progress to the next belt. I would never have imagined he could stand in front of an examiner and listen to what they were telling him to do, let alone remember and perform a sequence of movements while they watched him! Again, he is able to do something I had genuinely thought impossible for him when he started. This has been due to sheer hard work on his part, of course, but also the attitude and perseverance from his instructor. I will always be grateful to her.

There are some things requiring gross motor skills that he cannot do yet. He is still unable to cycle. For some reason this action is very difficult and uncomfortable for him. We have tried a few times to help him by putting our hands on his feet and helping him pedal. It appears to me that working out which way to apply pressure and which foot to use at different times is difficult for him. He does not like cycling and does not see it as fun, and although I think it may be good for him to learn to do it (as who knows what part of the brain he may 'activate' by being able to do this), I have abandoned it; there are only so many things that we can teach him and so little time to do it in. We pick our battles carefully.

We have also spent a lot of effort teaching him to swim. Getting him into the water was the biggest hurdle. I think it took at least a year to stop him being terrified of going in the pool. Again, this is not necessarily a trait that all autistic children share, as some love the water.   In order to teach him to swim, we would again have to physically move his legs and arms in the directions they needed to go. Just showing him was not enough. The doggy paddle was the easiest way to start.

Recently my husband has been trying to teach him the front crawl. The movement of lifting his arm out of the water and turning it to come down in front of him was very difficult for my son. We had shown him many times what to do and how to do it, but he just never seemed to pick it up. Often I thought it was simply because it was a difficult thing for him to do and he just did not want to try.

My husband, however, realised that although it looked like a simple movement to us, it required him to lift his arm and turn his hand down while it was up in mid-air so it could go around and down back into the water. For us this action was not difficult once we watched it being performed. For him it was almost impossible. First he would need to concentrate on the hand and notice the angle as it came out of the water, and then he would need to notice the hand turning in mid-air and work out how to do that, and finally he would need to remember what he saw and execute it. Every movement for him needs to be broken down into separate parts and processed, even though it looked like one fluid, easy movement to us.

My husband is now trying to teach him by moving his arm for him, explaining each action and why he is doing it. The frustration seems to be diminishing, and he is now able to swim that way for about ten metres on his own. He is able to swim 300 metres doing the doggy paddle, so it is obvious that the effort and concentration he needs to do the front crawl is tremendous, until he has practised it enough times and it becomes routine, as much for his mind as his body.

Playground equipment has to appear fun and challenging before he will try it. He has never enjoyed the swings and rarely sits on them for more than a minute. I think it is simply because he finds it boring. He is not a child who can generally sit in one place quietly anyway.

Climbing, however, he loves. Again, I think the combination of doing things like taekwondo and the piano has improved his sense of balance. He has gone on the 'aerial adventures' where children wear a harness and jump from plank to plank, walk on a tightrope, and that sort of thing. For someone who had no balance at all before, it is amazing to see him doing this and loving it.

CHAPTER SIX

FINE MOTOR SKILLS

Developing fine motor skills – anything that needs hand-eye coordination like picking up things, writing, drawing, doing up buttons, zips, and shoelaces, or using a knife and fork – is generally difficult for autistic children.

Before having an autistic child, I associated problems of fine motor skills with brain damage or injuries or with diseases such as Parkinson's. I supposed that as autism is a mental disability (a 'problem' with the brain), it would follow that autistic children would have the same symptoms as someone who had a brain injury. Treatment in that situation would include such activities as playing with putty (to strengthen the muscles in the hand), putting pegs in holes, threading beads, drawing, and painting.

These methods are great, but for an autistic child who may not like the feel of putty or doesn't really enjoy getting his hands dirty with paint, it may not be so easy. Autistic children also struggle to focus their minds, particularly if something does not interest them. Often, simply having no idea how to do something is enough to make my son walk away from it. Also, for my son, just sitting still to observe something was difficult. It was much easier to get him to do something that involved his gross motor skills, so I did not even try to make him draw and write when he was younger. He only started trying to hold a pencil just before he went to school. He ate mostly with his hands, and in a way this was good, because at least he was getting his hands dirty and getting used to different textures and moving the muscles in his hands.

I also wondered whether, in order to have good fine motor skills, we have to be aware of the task and visualise doing the task before trying it. That might explain his difficulty in executing each task, as he is not observant and is often not aware of a lot of things that happen around him, and visualising is a problem for people on the spectrum. Hence, the only alternative is to show him how to do something many, many times, until it is ingrained in his memory, and then perhaps he could eventually imagine doing it.

Getting him to concentrate on a task and not get up and move away from it meant being by his side throughout the whole task. He had to constantly be made interested in the task at hand. The task itself was not enough to motivate him to attempt or finish it. For example, with normal children, you could give them colour pencils, and the process of drawing and watching their picture come alive would motivate them to finish it. They would have an idea of what they wanted to achieve, work out in their mind how to go about achieving it, and then execute it with some level of confidence. With my son, he could not visualise what his painting or blocks would look like when finished, so he had no idea how to even start the task. Even showing him an end product of something would not help, as he could not imagine how he would slowly build up to the end product. Every step of the way, I needed to make up stories about what we were doing and how it would look in the end to keep him entertained and interested.

We always did simple things. For example, when using blocks or Lego, for a long time we would only build towers. He could not see how to do anything else, and there are so many variations of what you can do with blocks that I think it was too daunting a task for him even to try it. Repetition is the key to his learning, so changing the patterns of building blocks and complex Lego creations just did not help.

That was one of the problems in preschool; he could not do most of the things that the teachers were asking him to do. He would watch what other children were making and get angry and want to destroy it – probably from frustration. He would knock things off the table and laugh as he did it, making the teachers even angrier with him. I think that in his mind that was all he could do when faced with little beads and colour pencils. He needed someone to sit down with him, try and focus his attention, and show him slowly how to get started.

This is another reason to diagnose your child early and get a Statement. It was simply not possible for him to learn these things on his own. Also that Statement means that the people around him do not react with hostility and anger towards him. To all the reluctant doctors and specialists out there, surely it is far more damaging for a child to have the label 'naughty boy' rather than 'autistic'. People are far kinder to those with disabilities, even if not from compassion, then from political correctness.

When he was in Year 3 in school, his one-to-one teacher decided to take it upon herself to teach him to draw. She put so much time and effort into it. She is a wonderful, patient lady and actually managed to teach him by breaking down each part of a picture to show him how to draw. She must have spent hours teaching him to colour within the lines too. I had not spent much time on drawing and writing – I always imagined he would eventually learn to type on a computer – so this was one of the battles I did not bother fighting. It was wonderful that someone besides me would take it upon herself to teach him what he saw as such a difficult task. It is because of her perseverance that he now spends time drawing and colouring and actually enjoys it.

I believe that my son learns things in steps. If you imagine a graph with a stepped line rather than a smooth gradient, that would be how he learns. At first there is no sign that he can do a task at all, even though he has been looking at it and trying it for ages. Then suddenly it clicks into place in his mind what he has to do, and then he can produce something that looks like the end product.

One thing that I have not been able to teach him or encourage him to do is jigsaw puzzles. He says it is boring. I am not sure if that means he cannot do it and so will not try it yet, or if he simply cannot see the point of putting a broken picture together and then breaking it up again. Or perhaps it has more to do with identifying shapes. This is something I know he struggles with.

He now can write fairly well most of the time, but when he has to do a forward slash (/) or draw a triangle, he struggles with it. I would have to draw dots and tell him to join them. When I asked him to do it without the dots, he would not know where to start. It seems that joining dots is not a good way for him to learn. I know that it is something that lots of specialists recommend to start them off with writing and drawing. However, for my son, I think that joining dots becomes simply about concentrating on doing a straight line between the dots, and it might actually 'switch off' the part of his brain that makes him think about the shape he is drawing.

Instead, I would give him a blank piece of paper and talk him through it. I would have to say things like 'down towards the left' (fortunately he knows his left and right from piano and taekwondo), 'straight across', and so on. Verbal direction, although supposedly difficult for autistic children, seems to work here. Something to think about may be that there is no single rule for what is a good teaching tool. Sometimes visual teaching works best, sometimes verbal, sometimes physically moving their arms and legs. It all depends on what the task is and what the child seems to find helpful.

CHAPTER SEVEN

SPEECH & COMMUNICATION

Speech is another developmental milestone most children reach without much problem. Babies tend to babble around one year old, and parents are full of excitement hearing this incoherent attempt at conversation. By the age of two, toddlers are usually able to say a few words here and there, and if they cannot find the words, they are able to convey how they feel by gesturing, body language, eye contact, or expressions. By the age of three, most children are communicating with their parents with, of course, varying degrees of eloquence and vocabulary.

An autistic child, however, does not follow the same pattern. Not all autistic children will talk. Those who do talk may not always be understood. Their speech patterns are different. The content and the relevance of their conversations may often seem out of place and strange. Often they are seen as having conversations with themselves. They seem unable to grasp that the listener has no interest in what they are saying. They are happy to ramble on and on about their choice topic for hours, regardless of the responses, body language, or expression of the listener.

Another feature is that autistic people tend to take things literally. It is difficult for them to imagine that when a word is used in a phrase, that same word can translate to something completely different from its common meaning. For example, when my son was three and I said I would cut him a piece of cake, he would scream 'no cut' many times hysterically. It took us a while to realise that 'cut' to him meant to injure and bleed. When we replaced the word with 'slice', he was happy. Jokes and sarcasm too are beyond him, as the exact same words that mean one thing can have a totally opposite meaning just because of the tone and expression in which they are delivered. Even now, if I were to say an unfamiliar phrase like 'That is just great' in a sarcastic voice to something he knew was not a good thing, he would be very confused and ask me, 'Is it?'

My son skipped the babbling stage when he was baby. He did say a few words when he was two, but they were words he would mutter, and in no way was it a tool for communication. At three, he could name a few things. He would name them and then repeat them many times. He did not look at us when he named them, as he did not seem to care if anyone had heard him. It was as if he were talking to himself. He did not seem interested in sharing any thoughts with anyone. He did not try to draw anyone into any games he was playing. He would scream if he wanted something and did not get it, and we would have to guess what it was if he could not name it.

He called me Peppa from the Peppa Pig cartoon that he occasionally watched. (Yes, it was very flattering that the closest word he could associate with me came from a pink pig!). He refused to call me mummy for many months, even though I would correct him each time he called me Peppa. He did not bother to call his dad anything for a long time. His dad was just someone he would have to go to when Peppa needed a break from him. When he eventually referred to him by a name, it was George (Peppa's little brother)!

I remember that he was doing this around the time of his diagnosis. My husband and I were sitting in a room full of specialists, and we told them what he was calling us. They said that we should not play along with this as it would confuse him. They thought he actually believed we were the pig family.

This was easier said than done, and this was the first piece of advice about his speech that we rejected. First of all, although it was odd, at least he was acknowledging my existence (albeit as a pig, according to the specialist) and looking at me and including me in his world. Secondly, I felt that he had a reason for calling me Peppa, and I was sure he knew that we were not a pig family. Until today, I have no idea why he did it, but at the time I felt it was important to go along with it and simply encourage him to talk and say whatever he wanted, because at least he was talking.

He started speaking in sentences just before he went to school. Again, these were not really communicative sentences. They were more random observations. His words were difficult to understand, and only my husband and I, and sometimes his granny, who spent a day a week with him while I worked, could understand him.

The experts gave us lots of advice. The main thing was to keep speech simple. They really liked the idea of nonverbal tools like the PEC (Picture Exchange Cards) method. This system would work by having cards with pictures on them for him to show to us what he wanted, and we could use the cards to communicate back with him. This would mean that he would not be overwhelmed with processing a lot of words, and we would have a means of communication that could work both ways.

This seemed like a very good idea to me at first. Even with normal children, there are books and ideas about using sign language for babies to aid communication before they can speak. The thinking behind this idea is to remove the frustration babies feel from not being able to communicate.

So we tried it for a while, but with our son it did not work. He was not the sort of child that was interested in any sort of game, and I think he saw this as one. He would take the card and hide it somewhere, usually under the sofa. I was not particularly happy with this method either, as I actually believed that he understood what I was saying when he was concentrating on me. I also believed that he had a bond with me and listened to me, even if he did shut out the rest of the world at the time.

The first couple of years when he was in school, he would be visited by a speech therapist, perhaps a couple of times a year, for a few hours each time. They would always push for the PEC method to be used and appeared dissatisfied that we were using so many words and lengthy sentences with him. I am sure it was because the PEC method was thought to be a success with some kids who could not communicate at all. For them, it was probably a breakthrough, as they had gone from not having any means of communication to being able to express their wishes to everyone.

With regard to my son, I felt it was taking a step backwards. I am not saying that the PEC method is not a good one. I am saying that each autistic child is different, and experts should not stick to one tried and tested method from one particular group and suggest it should be the best way forward for every autistic child. We decided to carry on talking to him using sentences. We would try to make them easy to understand and explain as much as we could, but we always used sentences to talk to him.

I had a theory that it wasn't that he didn't understand me. I thought that with my son, the problem was that he did not focus and concentrate on anything that was going on around him. That meant that he did not absorb all the information available around him as other children did. He did not see or decipher anything on his own, because most of the time he would be in his own head, playing the way he wanted, ignoring the world around him. To me, that was very different from not being able to understand things, if he could just see and hear them. The fact that he could call me Peppa meant that when he wanted to, he could focus on things (like the cartoon), and he could apply what he saw somewhere else, albeit inappropriately.

My son had never been interested in toys or in doing anything other children did, so from the time he was a baby

I would talk to him about anything I thought he showed the slightest interest in. I thought that if I eventually explained everything (and I mean literally every single thing in the world that I could explain), then eventually he would understand how everything worked. It would take much longer with him than it would with other children, who are continuously taking in lots of things consciously and subconsciously, but I saw no reason why he could not understand things if he could just hear about them.

I would always start talking to him by calling his name until he looked at me, and eventually he would do this quite quickly. The type of 'conversation' I had with him was tailored to what he was interested in at the time. So in a way, he led the 'conversations'. I remember just talking to him about colours and numbers from a very early age. He very quickly learnt all the colours, and that made me realise that he could learn if he was focussed and wanted to. The same thing happened with numbers. When we went out for walks, I would point at the house numbers and tell him what they were, and he always appeared interested and seemed to take it in. He started to call out any numbers he saw from the age of four. I would also use numbers whenever I could in his everyday life.

I remember reading somewhere that there is too much going on in the world for those on the spectrum to take in. They hear all the sounds and see all the details, and it is difficult for them to prioritise what they need to concentrate on and what they need to block out. For example, when someone approaches them talking, they may be looking at the way her glasses shine when the light reflects off them, or the colour of her hair – my son always noticed hair, and there was 'good hair' and 'bad hair' – or maybe they would completely miss the fact that there is a person talking in front of them because the washing machine has changed its sound from a hum to a loud spin. My son at the age of four could tell me when the washing machine was about to spin by leaving the room just before, because the spin was 'too loud' and 'scary.'

All of the above may sound negative. It might sound like it cannot be good for people on the spectrum to have such keen observation skills for some things and no skills at all for others – especially if the keen observation skills are not on what we 'normal' humans see as meaningful. But actually, I thought it could be a gift. If he had the ability to focus on anything that interested him (for whatever reason), then perhaps he could learn all about it. If we could find enough things over time that interested him, he could learn a whole lot of things very well.

That was about the age I started doing the piano lessons with him. I also decided to start teaching him a little bit of Maths every day. I used to do things like give him a bowl of strawberries. (He loves fruit and always focussed on them without any prompting.) Then I would take away a couple and make up a story about how a naughty goblin stole them. (He sometimes paid attention to the Noddy cartoon and seemed interested in the goblins.) Then I would ask him how many they took, how many he had at the start, how many were left, and so on. If he bothered to answer and got it right, he would get the strawberries back. If he refused to look at me and answer, I would eat them! Sounds a bit cruel, but it worked, and I rarely got many strawberries after the first few times.

He is now very good at Maths. He feels good about it too, as he is aware that his classmates are impressed with his Maths skills. That feeling is what I believe will keep him interested. Perhaps he will even end up doing something with Maths in the future.

As he got older, he would chip in more and more in the conversations we had. We read a lot of books to him since he was a baby. Books were always something he liked looking at. We had hundreds of books, and he had his favourites. He would not say a word or repeat anything we said for a long time. When he was four, he could repeat lines he had memorised. I would always follow the words I read with my fingers. Sometimes he would too, but most of the time he would be distracted by the pictures. However, eventually he stopped looking at the pictures as he got used to them, so he could concentrate on the words being read. I would explain the words by using the pictures, and eventually he was saying random words and pointing to the picture that represented them. So in a way, we were using a picture method similar to the PEC method, but in a story version because that is what he found interesting.

Stories were the main way I conversed with him. As he got older (between the ages of four and five), it seemed that if I told him not to do something, he would ignore me and do it anyway, or he would do it and laugh. I think his social development was a couple of years behind the 'normal' kids, so it made sense that his rebellious years, instead of at the 'terrible twos,' came at four years old. Everything took longer for him to learn and develop, I am guessing, because he could only process a fraction of the information other children process at a time. So it made sense to me that his social skills would develop slowly too.

When he was in his rebellion stage, the only way I could get him to listen to me was to explain honestly the consequences of everything he did, no matter how scary it seemed (this I still do now). For example, if we were out, he used to be a nightmare and would just run away from me, and I would have to chase after him and catch him over and over again. He would pull away from me and try to go where he wanted, regardless of danger or how upset and angry I got with him. So when he was four and I knew he was listening to me, I explained to him about kidnappers. I told him why I always needed to see him and what could happen to him if he ran off. After that conversation, I never even had to hold his hand again. He always stays close enough to me that I can see him.

Of course, once our son has an idea in his mind, it tends to stick. A lovely elderly couple approached us once in a shopping mall when he was five and said a few words to him. He asked them if they were kidnappers. That was one of the few times I was glad he was so difficult to understand.

After that incident, I decided to try to teach him to read expressions. Again, I thought that if he could focus and I could explain every single expression, then he would understand them eventually. We would read picture books with laughing, crying, happy, and sad characters. I would need to explain stories where someone could cry because they were happy. I would make exaggerated expressions on my face too and get him to tell me what they meant. Of course, things like sarcasm still throw him, and every single time someone is sarcastic I will explain it. The good news is that he understands it after it is explained and will even find it mildly amusing. He will now also ask, 'Is that a joke?' if someone says something that doesn't make sense to him. I will explain how it is seen as funny, so he is learning about humour. He may not laugh and find it funny himself, but he is aware that others find it funny, and that to me is a big achievement for him.

We have never told him a lie, or at least not one where we could be caught out. The reason is that if we explain something incorrectly, he will remember it forever, and that may cause all sorts of confusion and distrust in future. When he was younger, I told him that Santa Claus was not real. He had heard about him from Christmas parties, songs, and stories and it really worried him. He was scared at the thought that a big fat man could somehow get into his locked house. When he realised that Santa Claus was not real, he was relieved and agreed to keep it a secret from other children. Unfortunately with some of the kids he particularly liked, he wanted to tell them what he knew. He was horrified that their parents could tell them such a scary lie. Out of the blue, he would deliberately bring up the topic of Santa Claus, sometimes months after Christmas, in the hope that somehow the children would find out the truth for themselves. It was a struggle for him not to tell them what he knew.

I also told him that he is autistic and different from the other children. I explained it by telling him that he is gifted in some things because his brain is special, but that other things were harder for him than they were for other kids. I told him how lucky he was to be autistic, as he has the ability to think and see everything differently. In the last year or so, I actually started believing it too. He is now very easy to discuss things with logically. He may not understand a lot of things on his own, but when things are broken down and explained to him, he is very logical, and recently he has even been asking a lot of questions about things that confuse him.

He sometimes gets upset when he speaks too fast and we cannot understand what he is saying. He speaks the way he reads – he misses out words and sometimes stutters and does not finish a sentence before he moves on to the next one. It is almost as if his mind has gone on to the next thing too quickly, before he can express what was on it. To me, it is like watching a conversation on TV fast forwarded, every so often pausing to hear the random word, and trying to put the story together. It seems as if his mind is not able to translate his thoughts into words fast enough before moving on to the next thought, and his sentences come out too fast and with gaps.

He will still babble on about anything that interests him without noticing that he is not really being listened to. His current obsession is dragons, and every game, story, and piece of work he does will have a dragon in it. At school he has to be told not to go off on a tangent talking about dragons if the focus is something else. He has to be constantly drawn back to the subject being discussed, but he will come back and he will do the work. At home we will also stop him mid-sentence if we need to.

If we do not need him to answer a question or to do some work, we let him babble on and will listen to his wild, unbelievable stories right through the day. Often we have to slow him down and make him repeat himself, as he is too fast and is unaware that we are not following him. Sometimes he will get cross with us for this, but we will explain each time that he is autistic, and we need him to slow down for us as he is too quick. There is very seldom quiet in our house with him continuously talking, but I am not complaining. I can remember only too well the day I wished and dreamed he would speak to me.

CHAPTER EIGHT

EMPATHY AND EMOTIONS

Empathy, to most of us, means the ability to share in the emotions and feelings of someone else. This would, of course, mean being able to understand and imagine what the other person is feeling by putting ourselves in the other person's situation. For some people, empathy is not just understanding what someone is feeling, but reacting appropriately and perhaps even providing support in some manner.

The general consensus is that people on the spectrum are not able to empathise. They are not able to understand other people's emotions. They are not even interested in other people. They are unable to offer affection and understanding, because they themselves do not crave or need it. They find it difficult to control and understand their own emotions (hence the temper tantrums when things do not go their way), so it would seem reasonable to assume that it is beyond them to identify with someone else or to put themselves in someone else's shoes.

I would disagree with all of the above, as I think my son is capable of empathy, and I would go so far as to say that he has more empathy than any other person I know! He also is a very loving little boy who needs physical contact such as hugs and kisses to thrive. What's more, he is aware of this need and often gives other people hugs and kisses if he likes them.

I did not always think this way, though. I remember, when he was a baby, thinking that his indifference to me – except for demanding I be around him all the time as his personal slave – was normal in all babies. All babies think the world revolves around them and are only interested in getting what they want. It was difficult to see if my son had bonded with me or if he just needed me as a constant in his life. It was difficult to determine if he could pick up on my emotions when I was stressed, because I was nearly always stressed, as he was nearly always stressed. We did not have those moments where we just gazed into each other's eyes, feeling the natural bond and overwhelming love of a mother and baby, the way the films show it (with moving music in the background).

However, when he was a toddler, it became clear that he did not care about making a connection with me. I remember hearing a couple of mothers saying how much they were enjoying watching their toddler grow and develop. My toddler was a growing nightmare. It became very clear to me that the reason I did not feel the same way as the other mothers was because I was not getting anything back.

Everyone talks about how it gets easier when your child starts to communicate and love you back. However, no passer-by would have picked up on this. No one at all in the 'mother and toddler' groups ever noticed that I was missing out. That was because my son would often be in my arms. He would be in my arms when I was catching him before he fell over and had an almighty tantrum. He would be in my arms when he was hungry. He would be in my arms when I would read to him or play with him because no other child wanted to. He would be in my arms because sometimes all he wanted to do was fiddle with a toy and he did not care where he did it – I was as comfortable a chair as any.

He never sought me out to show me anything he had done. Never brought a drawing or a toy to me to show me how excited he was. Never even came to me for sympathy when he got hurt. Basically, he never wanted to share any feelings with me.

On days when I was so tired after a bad night and day of tantrums that I would cry, he would not even notice. I remember sitting in my front room one day sobbing, and he just carried on playing. He looked up once at me, I think to see what the noise was, and turned away and carried on playing with absolutely no change to the expression on his face. No sign of distress. No show of understanding or interest. So, yes, all those articles and books that I read saying 'no empathy' was a symptom of autism, seemed accurate at that point.

Now, this may have been true when he was a toddler, but it started to change once we started being able to communicate with him. Once we started being able to tell him stories about 'good and bad'. Once we were able to break down and show him different expressions and body language of people who are happy, sad, etc. All he needed was for someone to explain to him what he saw. He needed to be able to identify that a certain expression or type of body language meant something. Above all, he needed to be able to actually see rather than just look – actually see and take in a situation.

I believe that when I was sitting there sobbing, all he saw was me sitting there making a funny sound that made no sense to him. He did not connect it to himself crying. I think he was simply not able to recognise, as other children do, that the sounds I was making were similar to the sounds he was making when he was unhappy. I do not even think he noticed the tears pouring down my face. Perhaps he noticed the colour of my sweater, or the way my hair was in a mess (he always had a fascination with hair), but maybe he did not even see my tears. That is what I believe anyway.

Here are some examples of why I think he has empathy in abundance now. Yesterday when I was sitting rubbing my head because I had a headache, he came up to me and kissed me on the head and said, 'What is wrong? You look like something hurts'.

If I ever hurt myself accidently, he will come running to 'kiss it better'. If I am annoyed that the house is in a mess, he will run around trying to tidy it up. If I am ill in bed, he will come to stroke my hair and ask me if I need anything. If I am carrying things that are heavy, he will offer to help.

It is not just me to whom he shows compassion. If a child falls over and cries, he will ask me to help him. If a young child he doesn't know is a little away from his parent in a shop, he will ask me to tell the parent before the child gets kidnapped! If he has a piece of fruit and there is someone near him without anything to eat, he will offer to share it with them. If his dad and I even raise our voices a little at each other, he will be there asking us to be kinder to each other. If he sees or hears about a child who has no parents, he is horrified and can even cry at the thought. If I want to kill a slug or spider, he is upset that I would hurt a creature that 'is not doing anything to hurt me'.

How did we go from what he was as a toddler to where he is now? Perhaps, as I said before, autistic children are just slower to develop emotionally compared to 'normal' children because of how much of the world they can take in at a time. Maybe things like empathy take a little longer to develop. Perhaps if they show no empathy for a longer period of time, it is difficult for other people to show emotions back to them as they grow older, and this becomes a vicious circle.

I for one know how difficult it is to feel warmth and love for someone who gave me back nothing for a long time. Not only is it difficult, sometimes this lack of affection translates into feelings of inadequacy and guilt for failing as a parent. Perhaps children on the spectrum pick up on this at some level. There are studies that suggest that children who are brought up in a hostile or unhappy environment may lack empathy and may fail to make good connections with the people around them. The same is said of children who grow up institutionalised, as they miss out on personal one-to-one affection and human attachment.

Again, please be very clear that I am not saying it is the fault of the parents or caregivers if their autistic children are not showing empathy. I am suggesting, however, that as these children are closed in their own world for a much longer time than a 'normal' child, it can be very difficult to show them what empathy means. Hence it is difficult for them to express it too.

I decided my son would be able to learn empathy from me as he seemed able to learn other things. I taught him empathy by telling him how I felt all the time. I would say things like 'I am angry or sad or hurt now because …' I would relate his feelings to mine whenever I could. For example when he was hungry, I would tell him I understood how he felt because my stomach was grumbling too. If he got hurt, I would tell him how lucky he was, because he seemed a lot stronger than me, and when I got hurt, I would cry. He seemed to like me identifying with his feelings. Eventually, he would copy what I was saying when he recognised the same situation.

He is able to transfer this understanding now to events he has never seen before at home. If he is watching a cartoon and someone dies, he gets very upset. If anything, I think he now puts himself into the other person's shoes more than your 'normal' child would and is affected much more.

As I was writing this, he came into the room. He was supposed to be asleep, and I am aware that the conversation we had was a delaying tactic. He asked me what I was doing, as he knows I like him taking an interest in things around him. Manipulation is not something a person is able to do unless they are able to assess the situation and understand how another person feels (the very skills needed for empathy).

I told him I was writing a book about autism. His response was, 'Oh cool [an expression learned from classmates], can I read it?' Reading for him is a chore, and he was only asking in order to keep the conversation going (more manipulation). I told him it was for adults.

'What are you writing now?' he asked. I told him it was about how he was difficult as a toddler and how he is so amazing now.

'That was because I was frustrated and could not understand things,' he replied. Those are my words he was copying. I asked him what age he was when he knew that he loved me. (As we are in the empathy chapter, I thought I might as well ask.)

He said, 'When I was three and a half'. I laughed at him and asked him why he came out with that age.

'Because you asked me,' he replied. I had to explain that I meant to ask how he arrived at exactly three and a half as the answer.

He said, 'Because before three and a half, I just did not love you'. I looked at him and asked him why.

He answered, 'Don't worry. It was not your fault. I just did not understand anything then.'

Now surely *that* is empathy – to try to reassure me. I am pretty sure he could not possibly know or remember when he started to notice and love me.

CHAPTER NINE

SENSORY OVERLOAD

Many parents of children with autism would be aware that they have issues with managing sensory inputs. In simple terms, signals from the five senses – sight, hearing, smell, touch and taste – are produced by the sensory organs (eyes, ears, nose, skin and tongue) and sent to the brain to be interpreted and understood. The brain needs to be able to identify this information and process what to do with it.

With autistic children, the first problem is whether their sensory system works the same way as that of a 'normal' person. For example, they might have acute hearing, where they could be hypersensitive to sounds. Some sounds that may be fine for a 'normal' child could be painful to them. Some colours or lights may make them feel very uncomfortable or scared. Some of them have very high pain thresholds, so they may hurt themselves before they realise that they should not be touching something hot or holding something sharp. Some of them may not be able to smell or taste foods that appear mild to the rest of us without feeling sick. Some may have all, perhaps more, of the problems above.

Just imagine that they do have these problems. Then it is reasonable that they would choose to cover their ears and hum to themselves or even scream to block out these sounds. If the lights are too bright, they may hide in their T-shirts or attack the source of light to get rid of it. Sometimes they may even rock or bang their heads against the wall to try not to 'see' and 'hear' these offensive stimulations. They may be unaware of the pain that we would feel as they bang their heads on the wall; it may actually be more comforting than facing the terribly painful sights and sounds that they are observing. To me, the issue is not that there is something wrong with them for reacting the way they do. The issue is that they have overactive or underactive senses. I felt that for my son the solution was somehow to reduce the impact of the senses he found overwhelming and to help him learn how to cope with the ones that were under-sensitive.

Assuming that we can find a way to deal with the over- or under-stimulation of the sensory organs, the next problem is whether the brain can decipher these signals once they have been passed to it, understand them, and then react appropriately to them.

So we are back to the issue of autistic people not being able to process efficiently information that they are receiving. Perhaps if there is too much going on, then processing input from various senses at the same time is impossible for them.

So I thought that the way to help him understand his senses was to isolate the things that upset him and to help him deal with each of them, one at a time.

My son has very acute hearing. He used to scream when we put the washing machine on and it went on 'spin'. It got to the point where he even knew when the washing machine was going to go into 'spin' mode and would get very agitated just before that happened. That means he knew from the sounds that the machine made what point of the wash cycle the washing machine had reached!

He used to cover his ears when we walked near a main road. He could not take the sound of a car whizzing by if it went more than about 20 mph. After hearing the smoke alarm go off once, he would be terrified of walking anywhere near it for days. If he saw a smoke alarm (or anything with a little red light), he would panic.

Certain things would make him go berserk if he saw them. The 'R' in the circle (the registered trademark symbol you find on everything) used to do that to him. He would scream 'Logo R! Logo R!' repeatedly, until we hid the object or the logo. Once he was in the bath and started to scream about the 'logo R'. My husband was frantically looking around trying to find the offending object. Finally my son pointed to a shampoo bottle, the back of which was covered with tiny writing. My husband tried to cover the letter R that he could see, but my son kept on screaming, 'Three logo Rs!' In one quick glance, my son had managed to see three tiny letter Rs within the paragraphs of tiny text that we couldn't see until we went through it line by line, scrutinizing the bottle slowly.

He would refuse to put on certain clothes because of their colours. If I forced an item of clothing on him (after all, he was only tiny; how hard could it be to pin him down and force his limbs through anything if I had half an hour free every day?), it would be off in seconds.

Just by looking at and smelling some foods, he would know that if he ate them he would be sick. Again, if I managed to get him to eat it through deception, he would retch and be sick with it immediately. The foods would not necessarily cause the same reaction each time. Sometimes the same food, cooked exactly the same way, would be fine. So it was not an allergy with him. He would go through phases of what he would eat. It was as if his body were telling him what he should eat and when. He would never touch anything with cream. He would not touch sweets (though that could be because he knew it was unhealthy, as we have always told him so).

He rarely knew if he had clothes on the right way around, even if they fitted badly. When he was five or six years old, he was encouraged to get changed on his own after PE in school. He would sometimes put his shoes on the wrong feet or have his pants on completely wrong. It would look so uncomfortable, but he never even noticed it, and trust me, if he had noticed that something was making him uncomfortable, everyone else would soon know about it!

He was terrified of vast amounts of water and would scream and scream the first few hundred times we took him to the pool. The noise in the pool, the number of people, and maybe even the temperature of the water were all factors here.

He hated getting his face wet, so putting his head underwater was out of the question.

He would go through phases of having habits that we would have to break. For example, one time when he was four or five years old, he was chewing the inside of his mouth, and he did it until he bled.

Solutions we tried to adopt did not work straightaway, and often we wondered if we were doing the right thing. No parent likes to do things that upset their child, and it is even worse when you are not sure whether you are doing the best thing for the child. However, we persevered because life was unbearable as it was.

Some things I could control, like the washing machine. I would put it on at times when he did not have to be near the room it was in. He would be aware it was on, but there was enough distance and enough doors in between to lessen the intensity of the spin. Little by little, I would leave things he wanted to play with nearer and nearer the machine. I would always tell him when it was going to spin (I learnt to work out when it would happen too!) and would suggest we leave the room, which he always chose to do. Eventually, however, he would anticipate the spin cycle himself and would leave the room quietly just before it started. In the last year or so, it has not been a problem, although sometimes I see him turning his head quickly to look at the machine when the spin cycle starts.

He has always loved walking, but we always had to walk a certain set route when he was little, or we would have a tantrum – every parent's favourite – at the side of the road for the whole world to see. (That was sarcasm. I would have to explain that to him if he ever read this book.)

To help him to cope with the sound of the cars whizzing by, we would tell him we were going to see traffic lights. From journeys in the car, we knew he was fascinated with traffic lights. So we would walk to them and sometimes spend an hour at the roundabout with six different traffic lights for him to watch change colour. We did this for about a year. We would do it in the sun, in the rain, in the snow, simply because he loved it and it was one of his favourite 'games'. Sometimes he would have us dance as we watched the lights change. Sometimes we had to run in between colours of some of the traffic lights. I am sure many commuters wondered why this crazy mother was always around the traffic lights forcing her poor child to do weird things with her. But it worked. He stopped being bothered by the sound of cars whizzing by. It was as if focussing on the lights blocked out the sounds.

We covered all the 'logo Rs' with stickers. We could not win that one. Over time he seemed to care less about them. Perhaps growing up and being interested in other things diminished their effect on him. Perhaps the part that piano and taekwondo played helped. I will never know. He still notices it now. Sometimes he will turn something around, and I will ask him why he did that, and he will say it's the 'logo R'. It is not a problem though, as he is dealing with it – quietly. Recently when I asked him what it was about the 'logo R' that bothers him, his answer simply was 'it just doesn't look nice'.

To get over tantrums about clothes, I just took him to buy whatever he wanted. I would never buy him anything with zips, as I was sure he would hurt himself. He still does not have a single buttoned shirt, and he only wears loose clothes. He still puts things on the wrong way and gets his shoes on the wrong feet. I have marked his shoes 'L' and 'R' as he just cannot see how they are different. I do not put the 'R' in a circle – I did this once by accident and will never do it again!

I mentioned at the start of this book that I let him eat whatever he wants. He will always eat tons of fruit. He will always eat enough from each food group that I do not worry about him getting everything his body needs. He is never tired or lethargic and very rarely gets ill. The only odd thing with his food is that sometimes he will want the same thing every day for a week. I am happy to go with this, as it does not do him any harm. Also, he has school dinners at school and apparently eats OK there, so giving him what he wants at home seems reasonable to me.

With the smoke alarm, we had to turn it off so that the red light disappeared. This would calm him down. Eventually we managed to help him understand why we needed it. However, that explanation caused a new fear that we needed to allay. His new worry was the possibility of a fire in our house, or in his school, or anywhere where he noticed a fire alarm; and we had to keep reassuring him.

We decided to join a gym where we had unlimited access to the pool. Besides the fact that it was a waste of money to go for just five minutes in a pool after paying for an hour, it was quieter to go to a less public place. I would take him for just five minutes at a time until he stopped screaming, and then I extended the time. When he was four years old, I put him in armbands and told him it was impossible to sink in them. After that, he would move around on his own confidently. Last year I got him some pink goggles. Pink is his favourite colour, so he loved them and put them on immediately. I had tried a few years ago to get him to wear goggles, but he absolutely refused. With the goggles, he was fascinated with going underwater, and that overrode the problem of getting his face wet.

Last year the girl of his dreams had swimming lessons in the pool he goes to. (He says he has loved her since he met her in his Reception class when he was four years old.) He noticed her there while we were in the water and asked us if he could take his arm bands off. Then he proceeded to do the doggy paddle without floats for the first time for 200 metres! This is what I meant earlier when I said his development appears to be stepped, rather than following a smooth learning curve. Maybe sometimes it is not that he cannot do it, so he just won't try; perhaps it is simply that he is not sufficiently motivated to try something new.

I stopped him from doing things like chewing the inside of his mouth by taking him to the doctor and getting some horrible cream for his mouth. After chatting with the doctor, I told my son that the doctor said that he would have to go to the dental hospital and have big blocks put in his mouth to stop him from chewing. The horrible cream and the thought of the big blocks in his mouth frightened him enough to stop chewing within a day. The harsh truth of actions and consequences really works on him.

In the last couple of years I have been able to take him to the cinema. That is something I would never have thought possible when he was four years old and still having tantrums, covering his ears where there was too much noise, and squinting at certain lights. The first film he went to see only lasted an hour, consisting of two half-hour Noddy films. It was a 'Kids AM' film, and the cinema was filled with young noisy kids anyway, so I was not too worried about having to take him out if he had a full-blown tantrum. I snuck in enough fruit in a bag to keep him entertained for the whole hour, and it worked. Unfortunately, it means that now, every time we go to the cinema, we need fruit. I explain to him what is going on throughout every film, so generally we prefer to watch a DVD at home. He has only developed the concentration span to watch a Disney DVD in the last couple of years. Before that, TV would only hold his interest for about four to ten minutes (the length of a Peppa Pig episode).

Whenever we watch anything on TV, I always watch it with him the first time. The reason is that if he is not able to follow it, he will 'switch off' and lose interest. Also, there is a huge amount of information that can be learned from a film, and the opportunity to explain things that he has an interest in is not something to take lightly. He has not watched anything beyond a 'U-certified' film, even though his peers are watching much more mature material. As he has not even asked or shown an interest in them, I am happy to stick with this for a while.

As I have said before, not all of these strategies will work with every child, and it is time-consuming and a very difficult process to try to reduce or eliminate the problems. Even now, there are things that he reacts to that other children do not even notice. The difference now is that we can explain why it is necessary to have these offending things around, and he seems to accept it – logic seems to prevail. Maybe he would have learned to cope with all these things over time on his own, but it felt as though we were doing something by coming up with strategies to help him.

CHAPTER TEN

CHALLENGES

I have written about my son's challenging behaviour right through this book. I think the general consensus is that autistic people are odd and difficult and socially impaired.

If a stranger had observed my son for any good length of time before the age of five, they would have said he was a child who was prone to random tantrums sparked by nothing in particular, isolated, unfriendly, uncaring, unresponsive, uncommunicative, incapable of learning, a danger to himself, and likely to become a danger or at least a burden to society when he grew older.

Anyone who was family or a friend could not, of course, have ever been so brutally honest or harsh. Often they only saw him when he had everything going his way (which, of course, he did when we had company). They would have thought I was a bit paranoid and eccentric and spoiling him at worst;

at best, they would have thought he was a 'normal' child who was just a little different and would grow out of it. I had some friends who were honest and expressed their fears, but even they were not sure, because my son did not tick all the boxes on the 'Is your child on the autistic spectrum?' test.

The boxes he did not tick that kept me hoping I was wrong about him were the following. He made eye contact with me. He loved to be held and cuddled (up to the point I could never get a moment's peace). He was saying a few odd words, and he had the ability to learn things like colours and numbers before any other child, so he appeared to be very bright. He loved listening to music (but only some, and there were some CDs he would scream to, which I would then never play again). He would look at books with me for hours. He would run around in soft play with me. (Of course, everything would be perfect before we left the house, and I would follow him and catch him every single time he almost fell, before he had a tantrum.)

I would laugh at him when he could not do something. I would make a joke out of everything that hurt to watch, because it was the only way I could make it through the day and not dwell on the fear that was gripping me and squeezing my hope away. Only my husband and I really knew what a nightmare we were living.

For a long time he did not bond with my husband. They did not have a good relationship until the last couple of years. However, this is apparently normal with babies and their dads. Nobody thought that it was odd that he would never show any signs of acknowledgement when my husband came home from work.

It was not as if his dad did not spend a lot of time with him every evening and on weekends, but my son did not seem to care or even notice my husband for years. He would tolerate him but would never seek him out. My husband would take him to the zoo every Saturday morning, just so I could get the shopping and washing done in peace. They would be together, walking the whole morning wherever my son wanted to in the zoo – usually the same places, and often to pick up leaves and stones rather than to look at the animals – but still he never showed any affection towards his dad.

Of course, we talked about the way he was and the things he was not doing, but for a long time, I did not tell anyone that I thought my son was autistic. When I expressed my fears to people who did spend considerable amounts of time with him, a lot of his behaviour was put down to us, his parents. My family would joke it was because I had been a difficult baby who always wanted my way, and he was pay back. My husband's family would comment on how my husband had liked his own space and time and had been a quiet child himself. It was too hard for them to consider seriously that something was not quite right. Also, my son could be extremely cute, so it was difficult for family to look at that image and see a 'mental disability'.

Even with his very difficult and odd behaviour, it took a lot of persuading to get him seen by the experts. I remember my last visit to a Health Visitor where my son came with me. Over a period of about a year, I had told various Health Visitors over three times, I think, that I had concerns that he might be autistic. We were in a room and, of course, my son was not interested in the toys that were strewn all around the room, as other toddlers were. After I had spent ten minutes trying to explain to her how difficult I felt life was, she told me that she could see how I was part of the problem. She said that while we had been talking, I had been hovering over him and following him around all the time and that I needed to let him go and just relax. She said that if he was having tantrums, part of the problem could be that he was picking up on my discomfort and unease of being a parent.

I think I was at the point of having a tantrum myself then, so I just sat down on the chair and watched him. Right on cue, my son fell over and, without me being there to catch him, bumped his head on the corner of something. He went into an almighty tantrum and was thrashing about on the floor. The Health Visitor started to look very concerned. I knew he could hurt himself, but I was at my wits' end and just numbly watched him. I asked her if she thought I should pick him up. She said yes. She continued that soothing him when he was upset was what I should be doing, and she instructed me to try to do it calmly so that he would calm down. So I held him very calmly as he tried to throw himself about, because (as he always did) he felt furious at being restrained while having a tantrum. He was three then, and he was incredibly strong even at that age. It must have looked like a wrestling match, as I am a small woman.

We must have sat there for about fifteen minutes. (She was lucky. He has had tantrums for up to an hour without stopping, and foaming at the mouth!) He was screaming in my arms, and I was just holding him while trying to have a calm conversation at the same time. Then he hit me in the teeth with his fist. Normally, when he had tantrums, I would pin him down with my arms and body to stop myself getting hurt too, and in our seated position, I was not on top form with my wrestling skills. Finally, she gave in and said something like, 'I think I will refer you on to the specialists'. She also gave me a leaflet to fill out to see if I was suffering from depression! I left at that point.

Not long afterwards my son had six weeks of observation by specialists and he was diagnosed as being severely autistic.

His behaviour got much, much better after he was five. He had a few tantrums in school, but nothing as bad as when he was at home. Maybe he never felt comfortable having tantrums there, or maybe he was distracted. Distraction never worked for us before the age of four. Reasoning was impossible, as he just did not hear us. For whatever reasons, perhaps all our strategies worked, after he was five, he was much easier to reach. We were able to tell him things. He still did not try to engage us or other children until, perhaps, when he was six, and then he did it awkwardly, but his behaviour did improve dramatically after that.

He seemed to care about getting praise as he got older. That was something that never seemed to interest him before he was six. Star charts and treats (even in school) did not have any impact until he was in year 2 (about six years old). He often would get angry but he would listen and take in explanations after he calmed down. He still gets frustrated very quickly, but he is now able to control how angry he gets.

His behaviour with other children varies quite a lot. There are some children who rub him up the wrong way, and he even goes so far as to make up stories about how naughty they have been. We know they are stories, because he will come out with things like, 'She burnt down the school today after the teachers caught her taking drugs on the roof.' I am pleased though that he is capable of lying, as that to me shows imagination rather than just imitation!

Generally, most parents and children are very tolerant and understanding of him. Occasionally there are incidents where 'lovely' children notice he is different and enjoy pressing his buttons. For example, in school there is a girl he says he loves. He has told me since he was four that he loves her. Every child in his class knows that he loves her, because he tells them all (including her) every day.

There was an incident when he was six where a couple of boys thought it would be funny to taunt him with 'She is dead' when they were in a playground after school. My son went completely nuts and attacked them. I always watch him (wherever we are, I am watching him), and I had to stop him fighting. For a while he was unable to explain what they said. His speech was not easy to understand, and until last year it was not easy for him to communicate, but when I did understand, I told the boys off. Children, however, are cruel. They did the same thing a few times more, and I ended up shouting at one of the boys. My son was placated by this, and I think I needed to do this in front of him to show that they were wrong to tease him. After that, we had lots of conversations where I explained that the only reason they did this was for a reaction. This really baffled him. He could not understand why anyone would do that. He has since learnt to laugh at people instead of responding with obvious upset or anger. This works, because his fake laugh is so scary that it would take anyone aback and stop them in their tracks!

It is difficult to address issues like this with some parents. I am aware that all parents have issues and fears about their kids, and no one wants to hear anything negative from another parent about their child. What I find interesting is that for some parents, the reaction to anything I say (as a mother of an autistic child) is one of trying to defend their child by saying that my son is too sensitive, and they will try to explain this to their child. I imagine there will be many incidents like this right through my son's life.

However, I never let him think that he is at fault for being upset about anything. I do, of course, make it clear that the solution is never to hit back. I have managed to convince him that he will be very dangerous one day if he becomes a black belt and that he could seriously hurt someone if he cannot control his temper. He does not like this thought, so he says he will learn to control his temper and not let things people say bother him. In some ways I think he is way more mature than a lot of children his age.

CHAPTER ELEVEN

ISOLATION

Isolation is something that people on the autistic spectrum tend to feel, due to their inability to connect with the world around them. I think for children on the spectrum this is not such an issue as it is for older people, as they seem to be happier in their own worlds. I think, as I mentioned before, that when they become teenagers, isolation and depression may become an issue. I am preparing to deal with that, and I will undoubtedly read a whole lot of books and, I hope, will find solutions to problems that arise when the time comes.

The isolation to which I am referring in this chapter is that which is felt by parents of children with autism. We may be surrounded by well-meaning, caring friends and family, but the sense of isolation and loneliness is nevertheless depressing and is rarely considered by others.

Before the diagnosis there is sadness and fear that is difficult to share, because it is such a horrific thing to say out loud about your child. Not only that, there were days when parents like me found it very hard to love their child. How could you possibly share this with other people? People may be tolerant about this for a while (for example with mothers suffering from post-natal depression), but when you struggle to like and love your child for years, it is difficult for any parent of 'normal' children to understand.

I remember my husband telling friends how difficult it was, how much we were struggling, and how people should really think about it before they had children. No one except me really heard the pain and hurt in the words he spoke. After a while, I did not want to hear what he was saying, because I felt hurt that he did not want my son. I felt guilty because I knew deep down that I understood exactly what he was saying. We felt that we had ruined our lives – that our happy life, as we had known it, was over. Even having each other, we were isolated and alone, as there was so much misery and emotion we could not come to terms with.

It was a huge relief to have the diagnosis, and it was definitely necessary for my son to thrive, but after the diagnosis, my world came crashing down again. Now I was alone, in the sense that all my friends have 'normal' children. There was the fear that we could not be a part of what they experienced. I was also terrified at the huge responsibility to help my child, now seemingly all on my shoulders. My friends would not be able to give me any advice about autism. They knew about the symptoms and some of the problems, but they would not need to think about the solutions I needed, in their day-to-day lives with their kids. They could talk about the problems they were facing with each other and be understood. I had no one except the experts. For a while I convinced myself that I could leave it all up to the experts. I would go with whatever they said, as they knew best and I knew nothing. It was easier to go with that idea for a while, because it took away the crushing weight of responsibility to get things right for my son.

I toyed with the idea of giving him up too. I remember one particularly bad day that sparked off this thought. I still remember it clearly. He must have had at least five tantrums that day (some lasting an hour) for various reasons. It was a day I was not working (I work part-time), and I was alone for most of the day, as my husband had to work late. I was desperate by the end of the day. I did not feel I could call anyone to help; no one could help even if they could come. I just watched him having tantrums, pinned him down, pacified him, and then repeated the process over and over again.

I had watched a programme on TV before my son was born, about a couple who had to put their autistic child in a special care home. I remember how his life as well as theirs was so much better after that huge painful decision. I remember them explaining how he was truly locked away in his own world. He had ADHD too. He needed routines that they just could not provide at home. I have no judgement about people who end up giving their child up. Sometimes it is the best thing to do for everyone involved.

I had many days with the idea rattling around at the back of my mind. I remember telling a friend, and she was sympathetic and great at listening, but of course she could not tell me what to do. I think if I decided to do this, my husband would, at that time, have gone along with it. But we never discussed it. We just struggled through each day, and things got better. Luckily, my son could say a few words; he could communicate sometimes when he wanted to. So he was probably very different from a lot of severely autistic children who are totally locked away. That made a huge difference.

I think it was a few months after the doom and gloom delivered by the specialists that I decided to start to think of ways to help my son. I had been talking to someone about her teenage son who was on the spectrum, and I asked her if she had just left it to the specialists and school to help her son. I was hoping she would say yes. She said no. She said she spent a lot of time helping her son to learn and develop. She said she did everything she could to help her son. That was when I decided I just had to do more. Hence all the strategies you have read about.

The way for parents to get through this isolation, I think, is to have a few good friends and family. I had friends with children the same age, and it was nice to be able to be a part of the lives of 'normal' children. It was never easy though. Very few people actually asked questions about how difficult it was. They had glimpses of moments of difficulty, but for some reason most people never really wanted to know much more. I probably was as much to blame, because it seemed that I was coping fine, and I supposed I was, as I was doing everything I could for him and never asked for help.

It is difficult to ask for help when you know exactly what it is that you are asking for. I remember wishing I could just have some time to go out for an hour to have fun. But how can you ask someone for this when you know what hell they will have while you are having fun? Before he was four, my son would not even go to my husband without screaming, particularly in the evenings. I would pass him to my husband to have a few minutes' peace in the shower, but his screams were so shrill and full of anguish that they used to penetrate the shower walls and torment me.

Eventually my husband and I decided we needed to do things for ourselves. He was four when we decided we needed to start living again. We would take turns going out in the evenings. Simple things like going to the gym made a world of difference to our lives. I cannot stress how important it is for a parent of an autistic child to have time to themselves. Somehow you have to find a way and not feel guilty.

Having friends to spend time with takes away the isolation a little bit. The time goes by a little faster. However, it was not necessarily less stressful. I noticed that as my son got older, there were more fights and quarrels, which are normal and part of growing up. However, often the children he had these disagreements with were articulate, while my son was not. Blame would often be placed on my son, and, of course, sometimes it was his fault.

I decided that I would have to be around to watch him every time there were other children about. Until the age of five, my son would hit back if something upset him. I had to watch so that I could stop him before it happened. Often I could see quite clearly why he wanted to hit them though. I have zero tolerance when it comes to hitting, and my son would always be told off if he tried to hit anyone.

I would make up stories to explain to him how bad it was to hit. The stories I would tell him would have the following elements. There was a lovely boy, but he could not control his temper, so he hit out at his friends when he got angry. He kept hitting them even though he knew this was wrong. He got so used to hitting that he could not stop even when he grew up. He lost all his friends. He got kicked out of school for hitting. He could not get a job. He started to steal, got caught, and was sent to jail.

Yes, that was the kind of story I would tell him! It was harsh and extreme, but for some reason that kind of story appealed to my son. He would listen to it intently, and, best of all, it worked!

There were a variety of reasons why my son would want to hit someone. Sometimes it was obvious. He would have a toy snatched away from him, and the other child would cry 'but I had it first' (that wonderful gem), and my son would hit the other child repeatedly. Nobody would notice the toy being taken, but you can be sure they'd notice the hitting and the other child in tears, so it is not difficult to see why parents would blame my son.

Sometimes it was less obvious. For example, a certain sound from a toy or other noise would upset my son. The 'normal' child would notice it. We know how lovely children can be (all children, including those perfect ones and those on the spectrum), and the 'normal' child would keep making the noise, enjoying the power he had to get a reaction. Again, I am aware that all this is part of growing up. The problem is that parents of 'normal' children would not see their child as doing anything so wrong as to warrant getting a thump. They could not see this assault on my son's hearing as being so bad. My son on the other hand, I am sure, would think that thumping the 'normal' child to stop assaulting his eardrums, was a fair exchange of pain.

My only solution to this problem was to watch everything. I would stop a lot of hitting by my son before it happened. I would glare at the child who thought it was funny to torment my son. Doing this all the time meant that I would isolate myself from conversations that the other mothers were having. Don't forget that if my son left the room they were in, I would have to follow. Otherwise, there would be that almighty tantrum if he fell or got hurt, and I would have to make a hasty retreat anyway.

The other thing I noticed was that if anything was broken, or there were incidents like writing on a wall, my son would be blamed. Parents would have a quiet word with me. Some of the time, they would be right. For example, my son loved to take tiny toys that he could hold in his hand and hide them under the duvets or pillows in the houses he went to. He would do this with quick and subtle moments when I went to the toilet for a few minutes – quite clever, really, when I think about it now. He could get around everyone, child and adult, to do this without being caught. However there were times when I knew he was not at fault. For example, drawing on a wall before a certain age was beyond him, and he hated holding pencils too. Being quirky and different made him an easy target for blame when there were any incidents.

Most of my friends just accepted that I needed to be around my son. However, few would follow me around, and I could not blame them. The whole idea of meeting up was for a break to have a cup of coffee while the children entertained themselves.

It was difficult to have family outings too with children of the same age (when my son was under the age of six). The reason was that most children would be interested in the animals in the zoo, or the games that they would make up, or walking with a purpose, whereas my son would be fascinated by a stick instead of the gorilla in front of him. He would squat down and look at a hole in the ground instead of playing with a ball. He would walk only where he wanted to walk, rather than stick with the group.

Again, everyone would be tolerant and accepting, but they would of course move on, as their kids would be excited about the purpose and the point of the outing. I found those days very stressful. I put us through it because I thought it would be good for my child to be surrounded by 'normal' children and 'normal' activities, even if he did not really seem to be a part of it.

Even at the school playground after school, I would have to watch him play (as I explained in the previous chapter) to prevent incidents. I think perhaps parents thought I was unfriendly and not sociable. I did not mind not being part of the social school groups that parents make up, but it was another place where I felt isolated (even if it was voluntary). Kids would be invited to each other's home for tea after school, but my son never was. I was not keen on inviting anyone back either, as my son of course showed no interest in that until the age of 6.

There are also incidents that make you feel alone. For example, something as simple as taking my son to have his hair cut was impossible for years. He went to an 'experienced with children' hairdresser, and she ended up coming out of the shop to try to cut his hair outside, as he got so very distressed. The look on her face when we left without managing to even snip one strand of hair was awful. I would cut his hair in his sleep – a snip here and there wherever I could. Fighting with him with a pair of scissors when he was awake just did not seem like a sensible idea. Often a friend would notice the end product of my talents, and a comment about how I had no skills as a hairdresser would be made.

Buying and fitting shoes was another nightmare. No-one could understand how a child can be so upset about doing something as simple as this. They are shocked, and some looked annoyed at the tantrum that ensued when we tried to fit a pair of new shoes on him. Fortunately, we managed to keep him in shoes once we forced them on, because he just did not have the dexterity to get them off. Certain shops offer appointments to fit autistic children with shoes before their official opening times. I never took them up on it, but in hindsight I should have.

Now things are very different. Today he will play with other kids quite happily. He prefers to play imaginary games or games that involve running or jumping. He always plays cheerfully with younger kids, which I think makes sense, as I believe he has matured more slowly than kids his age. He always seems to play better with girls. They are typically far more accepting, will listen better, and are less aggressive. Anyway, I prefer my son not to play with any child who hits, and boys do tend to do that more often. My son now is actually a very loving and affectionate boy. He has no problem telling a girl that he fancies her. Usually this causes a lot of giggles from a group of girls, but at this stage in his life, this is not a problem as they accept him and think it is funny and enjoy teasing him about it. He does not mind this, because he thinks they are funny for making such a big deal of it.

As for being isolated, in the past few years I have accepted I do not need to be part of a group who have children playing together happily. I have some very good friends who have helped me through very difficult periods without even realising it. I have one friend who I see quite often, just her and me without kids. There is no pressure, and I am able to talk freely about my son and she is always interested in his progress. I have another friend who is much amused by his Maths skills (see next chapter), who is always excited and happy for what he can do, and who loves quizzing him. She makes me smile with her enthusiasm. My mother and I email every day about little details in his life, and although she always thinks he is amazing and perfect, this does not bother me now as things are not difficult. My mother-in-law will spend a couple of hours playing with my son every Sunday so that my husband and I can switch off. I have found a new friend who is extremely supportive and accepting of my son, so if and when it all gets difficult during puberty, I am sure she will be there for me. I am grateful for all these people in our lives.

Strangest of all, I have friends whom I write to on the Internet who are so far removed from my life that they end up giving me some of the best and most supportive advice. One of them suggested that I join the taekwondo classes myself to help my son when he gets frustrated. That was great advice. Besides enjoying it myself, it makes my son extremely happy to watch his mother struggle with coordination and constantly go the wrong way. Another Internet friend has been really encouraging about writing this book, and this has helped me tremendously too, because even if it does not help anyone else, it has been very therapeutic to express all the past hurt and pain in words.

To conclude this chapter, what I want to say is that the life you have (especially if your autistic child is your only child) can be isolating. I cannot stress enough that in order to survive the very difficult times, you need to do whatever you can to find the people, the interests, and the time for yourself to make you happy.

CHAPTER TWELVE

BRIGHT SIDE

Yes, that is the title of this chapter! There is a bright side to being on the autistic spectrum! Despite the rough beginning and all the hard work (behind me and ahead), there are things about my son that I see as special and wonderful and I am so proud of. This final chapter is about what my son is like now, and I hope it will give you some hope.

He is very easy to reason with. He is very logical, and even when he gets frustrated, he is easy to calm down. From the time he started to listen (somewhere between four and five years old), we have been talking and telling him stories to teach him as much as we could. Previously in this book, I talked about how I was determined to tell him anything and everything so that the world would not be so confusing to him. Well, the amazing thing is that because of this resolve, I have probably talked to him and broken down more things than most parents of 'normal' kids have. My husband says I never shut up where my son is concerned.

The result is that we talk about everything. Often he will talk about dragons and things that are not of interest (to anyone!), but he will now ask questions too. In the past my husband and I would talk to each other while our son was in the room without changing our speech to take account of his being there. We just assumed he wasn't paying attention, so we could talk freely and not worry about what he might 'pick up' from our conversations. A couple of years ago he would rarely listen to us, even when we were addressing him directly, unless we called his name a few times first to direct his attention. A few months ago we were talking, and he interrupted to ask us a question about what we were saying. That was amazing. Last week he was in a different room, and he came in to join in our conversation. These are all things we never thought would ever happen. For some reason, he is beginning to take an interest in the world around him.

In the last year we have even talked about how he might change as he grows up and hits puberty. I have a lot of fears about that age for him, as there is so much literature about how adolescence is particularly difficult for kids on the spectrum, because their 'social disability' makes them vulnerable. I am worried that he will struggle to interact with his peers and that it will become painfully apparent to him then. I am preparing him now for it by telling him how different he is and how it is 'cool' to be different. I am preparing him for being bullied by encouraging him to get to a higher grade belt in taekwondo, in the hope that kids, just knowing he is able to defend himself, will leave him alone. I am preparing him by telling him about how teenagers can be mean and unkind simply because they think they are acting grown up when they are not. I am telling him that it is good to be different and to realise this. I am even telling him that teenage girls may have a preference for 'bad boys' and he must not be upset if the girls he likes do not give him the time of day. I am telling him that they will come around when they get older and realise how amazing he is. I am telling him about drugs and alcohol and peer pressure.

He has taken all this information in his stride. I remember telling him about peer pressure and about being manipulated into taking drugs (using much simpler language, of course), and I told him about how some people may even hide drugs in sweets to make them look enticing. His reaction to this was to express with horror, 'Drugs *and* sweeties? *Two* bad things?!!'

My son has a gift with Maths. I know that not all children on the spectrum have gifts. However, I do believe that they have the ability to focus on things that they find interesting, and that may lead to them being very good or even exceptional at certain things. I have always spent time with my son doing Maths questions, as he seems to enjoy them. He kept getting better and faster at solving numerical problems, so I kept finding more difficult and challenging questions for him to do. He and I spend about ten minutes a day now doing Year 7 Maths questions. My son is in Year 4. He struggles with any of the Year 7 Maths questions involving spatial awareness (for example, shapes and rotation), but he easily solves anything to do with numbers. We are hopeful that if he keeps improving and enjoying Maths, one day he could find a Maths-related job – something we never thought he could do when he was four!

The way he makes it easy to talk about everything is a bright side. If something makes sense to him, he will accept it. He knows that some things are difficult for him, and I have told him the only way to do them is to work hard. Sometimes he is in tears because he cannot imitate a taekwondo move, but the bright side is that he will work at it until he can. Sometimes he gets frustrated because writing and reading is difficult for him, but he will persevere because he has in his mind that it is worth working hard for anything you want. This does not mean I do not have to remind him and constantly push him. I do, but he will work hard without grumbling.

I do not think he has a mean bone in his body. (That would be a difficult sentence to explain to him!) The bright side is that even though I have mentioned that he can say things which are untrue and manipulative to some small extent, I do not think he is capable of ever intentionally hurting someone. As I said earlier, he has more empathy than any child I know. We no longer have any tantrums, because he knows it would upset us.

He is a very healthy child, because he is aware of the things that are not good for his body. We told him about sweets not being good for his teeth, and he steers clear of them. He loves exercise, and I think that the reason is partly because he knows it keeps him healthy.

I can truthfully say that I wouldn't wish that my little boy was any different. I do hope that life will not be hard for him and that he will find his place in society as he gets older.

I do hope that he will find good friends who understand and care about him. I do hope that he will be able to hold down a job, put his shoes on the correct feet, and zip his trousers up when he is an adult. I hope that the journey from childhood to adulthood does not scar him too much. But most of all, I hope that I will always have the close relationship I have now with my wonderful little boy forever.

ABOUT THE AUTHOR

Renitha Tutin came to the UK from Malaysia when she was 20 years old, having been awarded a British High Commissioner Awards Scholarship. After graduation, she went on to qualify as a Chartered Accountant. She left industry after her autistic son was born and now teaches part-time at the University of Bristol, devoting the rest of her time to him.